W9-DHX-722

ideals MOTHER'S DAY

More Than 50 Years of Celebrating Life's Most Treasured Moments

Vol. 52, No. 3

*"Mother—the essence of loveliness,
the beauty of a rose, the sparkle of a dewdrop,
and a sunset's sweet repose."*

—*Lydia M. Johnson*

IDEALS—Vol. 52, No. 3 May MCMXCV IDEALS (ISSN 0019-137X) is published eight times a year: February, March, May, June, August, September, November, December by IDEALS PUBLICATIONS INCORPORATED, 565 Marriott Drive, Suite 800, Nashville, TN 37214. Second-class postage paid at Nashville, Tennessee, and additional mailing offices. Copyright © MCMXCV by IDEALS PUBLICATIONS INCORPORATED. POSTMASTER: Send address changes to Ideals, PO Box 148000, Nashville, TN 37214-8000. All rights reserved. Title IDEALS registered U.S. Patent Office.

SINGLE ISSUE—U.S. $4.95 USD; Higher in Canada
ONE-YEAR SUBSCRIPTION—8 issues—U.S. $19.95 USD; Canada $36.00 CDN (incl. GST and shipping); Foreign $25.95 USD
TWO-YEAR SUBSCRIPTION—16 issues—U.S. $35.95 USD; Canada $66.50 CDN (incl. GST and shipping); Foreign $47.95 USD

The cover and entire contents of IDEALS are fully protected by copyright and must not be reproduced in any manner whatsoever.

Printed and bound in USA by The Banta Company, Menasha, Wisconsin. Printed on Weyerhaeuser Husky.

The paper used in this publication meets the minimum requirements of American National Standard for Information Sciences—Permanence of Paper for Printed Library Materials, ANSI Z39.48-1984.

Unsolicited manuscripts will not be returned without a self-addressed, stamped envelope.

ISBN 0-8249-1125-3
GST 131903775

Cover Photo BOUQUET OF LILACS Al Riccio, Photographer

Inside Front Cover SPRING FLORAL Pat R. Enk, Artist, under license of Sunrise Publications Inc.

Inside Back Cover MOTHER AND CHILD Jesse Willcox Smith, Artist. From the collection of Thomas L. Cathey, under license of Sunrise Publications Inc.

Memories
of First Spring Blossoms

Caroline Darr Fitzsimmons

Far away in wooded fields,
'Neath the grass and mosses
Sleeping,
Nestling so still, so low,
Little heads are shyly peeping,
Waiting for the snows to go;
Violets, mayapple blossoms,
Forget-me-nots that you loved so.

They bring back childhood days to me;
School hours over, oft I
Gathered,
Mother, these sweet flowers for thee.
O'er hill and bank of stream I wandered;
To part from thee I never thought.
Dear to me are first spring blossoms,
Dear the precepts that you taught.

2

LUPINE AND MONKEY FLOWERS
Mt. Hood Wilderness, Oregon
Steve Terrill Photography

A Garden Memory

Lillian C. Busby

The garden holds in its embrace
Fresh floral charm and willows' grace.
Shy, angel-winged begonias laze
In shade and cheer the human gaze.
The larkspur gay grows shapely, high;
A wren bird seeks her house nearby
And shares her evening melodies
Above mute garden rhapsodies.

There roses—God's most gallant things—
Without a soul or voice that sings,
Unfold with pride for all to see,
The owner, neighbor, friend—all three.
And all are blessed because they grew
As Nature destined them to do;
There birds and bees and scented flowers
Commune in silent golden hours.

Overleaf Photograph
BELLINGRATH GARDENS
Theodore, Alabama
Gene Ahrens Photography

SUNDIAL WITH ROSES
Dick Dietrich Photography

Dew

Patience Strong

Strolling through my garden before the sun was high,
I thought I saw a diamond—its dazzle caught my eye—
In the untamed jungle behind the tidy beds,
Somewhere in the tangle of docks and thistle-heads.

A flashing, fiery pinpoint of iridescent light
Picked out by the sunshine in colors clear and bright,
A rainbow-tinted jewel that sparkled gloriously.
Was it real, I wondered, a priceless find for me?

And so I went to seek it, down where the wild weeds grew,
Only to discover it was a drop of dew.
From the worldly standpoint, I found a worthless thing,
But it was far more lovely than the diamond in my ring.

Opposite Page
DAHLIA BLOOMS REFLECTED IN DEWDROPS
Steve Terrill Photography

From My Garden Journal

by Deana Deck

LAVENDER

Whenever I catch a whiff of lavender, the same vivid picture comes to mind. It doesn't matter whether I'm strolling through an herb garden, browsing through a fragrant soap-and-lotion shop in the mall, or walking past a potpourri booth at a craft fair; I am instantly transported to the stifling hot summer days of my childhood on the Oklahoma prairie.

Instead of summer camp, my cousins, brother, and I spent most of every summer visiting our grandparents' farm. One of our favorite pastimes was sliding down haystacks or, better yet, leaping from the loft door onto a thick, soft pile of new-cut hay. We could while away the entire day building hideouts in the hay and attacking or defending them, depending on whether we were the good guys or the bad guys that day.

And then we'd start to itch. Eventually my grandmother would haul us indoors, and we'd each get our turn soaking in a giant, old-fashioned tub of lukewarm water and baking soda, liberally permeated with lavender-scented bubble bath. The soothing effect of the bath and the calming fragrance often rendered us too drowsy to protest as we were led away in huge white towels, slipped deftly into clean pajamas, and tucked in for a quick nap under cool, lavender-scented sheets in front of a gently whirring electric fan.

My grandmother smelled of lavender year-round. She must have been partial to lavender water or oil, but at the time I just thought that was how she naturally smelled. She was typical of her time and kept lavender sachets in all the linen closets, lingerie drawers, and blanket chests. When I recently received a gift of lavender soap, I discovered the pleasures of aroma-influenced time travel and realized that the scent that haunts my childhood memories is that of lavender, sweet lavender.

Lavender dates back to ancient Egypt where it was used for medicinal purposes. In the Middle Ages it was considered an herb of purification, love, and protection and was thrown on midsummer night bonfires to bless the summer solstice. Today's soaps and bubble baths are just a modern adaptation of one of the herb's other ancient uses—as an oil to perfume the baths of noble Romans, Greeks, and Persians. Fortunately, lavender was so easy to grow and so widespread that its use was not limited to the nobility for very long. Peasant cottages were made more livable by the use of lavender sprigs strewn among the rushes that covered the dirt floors.

Queen Elizabeth I of England was quite fond of lavender tea and decreed that lavender conserve, used to flavor fruit and roasted meat, should always adorn her dining table. The Sun King, Louis XIV, carried fresh sprigs of the herb with him at all times and always bathed in lavender water. It is thought that the very name itself, *lavender*, derives from the Latin word *lavare*, to wash.

Lavender was one of the herbs that made its way to the New World with the Pilgrims and all across the frontier. Pioneer housewives often dried their linens by spreading them across huge lavender shrubs.

Most species of lavender come from the Mediterranean area, but others are native to islands in the Atlantic Ocean, areas of Asia Minor, tropical Africa, and parts of India. As a result, there are types of lavender that can be grown just about everywhere.

What we think of as "true," or English, lavender is *Lavendula agustifolia*. This is the lavender used to distill oil and fragrances. Royal chemists and purveyors of lavender essences actually designated it as *L. officinalis* to distinguish it from other less fragrant forms of the plant.

Dozens of cultivars of lavender exist, including the so-called Italian or Spanish lavender (*L. stoechas*) and the spike lavender (*L. spicas*). The bunches of lavender sold by florists are usually French lavender (*L. dentata*), which is available in the United States year-round because much of it is grown in Australia.

Although lavender has given its name to the pale purple color commonly thought of in relation to the plant, a wide variety of colors is available, ranging from white to mauve and from blue-gray to deep purple.

All species of lavender are highly fragrant, but what is seen most frequently in the herb garden is related to *L. agustifolia*. When dried, this species retains its fragrance for years rather than three to six months as other varieties.

Lavender is the lazy gardener's dream plant. It likes dry weather, has few disease and insect problems, and its foliage retains an attractive appearance after blooming, unlike many other perennials. When planting lavender, keep in mind that it is native to Mediterranean regions and prefers slightly drier conditions than other garden plants. In fact, hot, dry conditions contribute to the production of the most fragrant oil. Since lavender's native habitat is somewhat sandy, provide fast-draining, light soil in a full-sun location when planting.

Lavender is evergreen in warm climates but will survive cold weather where winter temperatures drop no lower than zero degrees Fahrenheit. If you live in a climate with colder winters, you'll be glad to know that the many dwarf varieties are easily grown in containers. Some cultivars, such as the English "Alba" hybrids, are not as cold hardy as the species plants and will benefit from added protection during the winter months. Full shrub forms and newer dwarf varieties of lavender make it easy to select a type for your particular needs. Smaller varieties grow nicely in rock gardens or as clipped border hedges, and the huge, unpruned "grandmother bushes" provide a dramatic focal point to any garden. To rejuvenate these bush varieties in spring and to keep them from becoming straggly, cut them back in April.

Lavender can be started from seeds that many catalogs offer but is more easily propagated from stem cuttings or root divisions. Most garden centers that sell herbs and perennials will usually offer lavender, but if you can't find plants locally, they are available by mail.

Although lavender-scented sachets do not infiltrate my entire house as they did Grandmother's, I will always keep a bit of lavender around to remind me of the sunny days of my childhood and Grandmother's loving care.

Deana Deck lives in Nashville, Tennessee, where her popular garden column is a regular feature in The Tennessean.

The Garden Entertains

Abby Westenberg

The garden was dressed in a silvery light,
Aware of her duties as hostess that night.
Her face wore the smile that she best could assume;
She had on her sweetest and rarest perfume.

Her house was a glorious riot of bloom,
For hundreds of blossoms filled up every room.
The floor had a carpet of velvety green,
The softest and richest of rugs ever seen.

A fountain's soft musical murmur so clear;
The orchestra hired to lend atmosphere.
The lighting effect with all else was in tune;
'Twas furnished by faithful, romantic old moon.

Two guests were invited to dine there that night,
And soon after eight by the hourglass bright
A boy and a girl from outside in the gloom
Stepped into that beautiful fairyland room.

They strolled to a half-hidden, moss-covered seat,
Stood, just for a moment, their hostess to greet.
Then, seating themselves, they proceeded to dine
On delicate morsels and potations divine.

And when they had drunk and had eaten their fill,
The spell of their hostess surrounded them still.
But suddenly, in an excitable state,
They cried, "We must go, it is getting so late."

Their hostess, the garden, smiled just as before,
And lovely as ever she went to the door.
And then in the midst of her silvery light,
Her guests bid their wonderful hostess goodnight.

Beauty That Endures

Mary E. Linton

The wild crab tree lives all year long
For one brief hour of May
And bears its thorns and bitter fruit
When blossoms fade away.

Still when we think of wild crab trees,
We think of loveliness
And vision in our memory's eye
Pink clouds of Maytime dress.

So we forgive a world of faults,
Remembering what is best;
For beauty rooted in the soul
Surpasses all the rest.

The Beauty of Trees

Wilson Flagg

It is difficult to realize how great a part of all that is cheerful and delightful in the recollections of our own life is associated with trees. They are allied with the songs of morn, with the quiet of noonday, with social gatherings under the evening sky, and with all the beauty and attractiveness of every season. Nowhere does nature look more lovely or the sounds from birds and insects and from inanimate things affect us more deeply than in their benevolent shade. Never does the blue sky appear more serene than when its dappled azure glimmers through their green trembling leaves. Their shades, which in the early ages were the temples of religion and philosophy, are still the favorite resort of the studious, the scene of healthful sport for the active and adventurous, and the very sanctuary of peaceful seclusion for the contemplative and sorrowful.

FLOWERING CRAB APPLE TREE
Green Bay, Wisconsin
Darryl R. Beers Photography

15

WHITE LILAC. Michael Olenick. F-Stock Photography.

LILACS AND MAGNOLIAS

I have often thought that two particular flowers are especially appropriate for Mother's Day—the lilac and the magnolia. Whether you live in the North or the South, you can enjoy the beauty of one of these flowers on this special day.

During my years in the North, I picked the lilac for its beauty and fragrance. There the lilac reaches its prime of bloom from mid-May on. I can't select the lilac in the Blue Ridge foothills where I now live because my dooryard lilacs blossom in early April, a full month or more before the observance of Mother's Day. But in the North, our family kept bouquets of lilacs in the house on Mother's Day and during their entire season of bloom. We had the loveliness and fragrance of the blooms all throughout our home.

We also had a lane of lilacs along an old

SAUCER MAGNOLIA. Magnolia Soulangeana. R. Todd Davis Photography.

stone wall that led from the dooryard to the barns. Another old lane of blooms stretched from the barn to the creek. I once planted more lilacs along the creek itself and on a steep creek bank in the edge of the woods. Some years later, they had spread into an unused pasture on the opposite side of the creek.

For Mother's Day in the South, I select the loveliness and aroma of the magnolia. Every year several large, aromatic magnolia blooms grace the tabletops throughout my home.

The magnolia is a charming tree that puts forth its large, waxy flowers in the month we honor our mothers. It is both a tree of beauty and a tree of song. I have listened to the humming of the bees as they moved from blossom to blossom. I have also enjoyed the lilting chords and carols of birdsongs from the mockingbirds, brown thrashers, robins, and cardinals. I am always inspired by the music of the birds, the whispering leaves, and the opening of the magnolia's large, white or pink flowers.

Each May for the past twenty-five years, my love for the Creator's Carolina hills has been enriched by the beauty and charm of the magnolia. The beauty of the flower and the season lead me to sing the precious songs bestowed upon me by my mother, rhythmic songs and lullabies that will forever linger in my heart. In memory of her, I shall always treasure the lilac and the magnolia.

The author of two published books, Lansing Christman has been contributing to Ideals *for over twenty years. Mr. Christman has also been published in several American, foreign, and braille anthologies. He lives in rural South Carolina.*

Lilac Time

Iris W. Bray

When lilacs perfume May's sweet mist
   And spin their fragile lace,
'Tis then I feel her presence most
   And sense love's warm embrace.

For fragrant lilacs were her choice
   From spring's enchanting bowers;
In close rapport she speaks to me
   Through language of the flowers.

At lilac time, in sweet bouquets,
   Fond memories I trace
And find within their loveliness
   My mother's smiling face.

LILACS
H. Armstrong Roberts

On Wings of Early Morning

Georgia B. Adams

On wings of early morning
Oh come and glide with me
And catch breathtaking glimpses
Of springtime's pageantry.

The daffodils, still dew-swept,
Rub their sleepy eyes;
Seeing us so early comes
To them as a surprise!

The robins, sweet, winged creatures,
Are sounding forth their praise;
From treetops near and distant,
We hear their roundelays.

On wings of early morning,
When day is at its best,
Share all its lovely freshness;
Come now and be my guest!

COLLECTOR'S CORNER

Lisa C. Thompson

COLLECTIBLE WOMEN'S HATS. Jerry Koser Photography.

HATS

Extinct fashions often make popular—although not always lucrative—collectibles. Like the folding fan, buttonhook, and lace handkerchief, hats have lost their place in the fashion world but gained status as a charming collectible.

Since hats were such an essential part of the everyday wardrobe for both men and women from the late 1700s until the 1950s, styles changed almost as often as people changed their clothes. Stylish hats were particularly at the height of fash-

ion from about 1890 until about 1930, which makes the deerstalkers, boaters, and picture hats from this period desirable to many collectors. The fashion death of the hat has been attributed to the popularity of casual fashions for both genders in the late 1950s, but for women's hats, an even deadlier culprit has been identified: hair spray. The towering hairdos of the late 1950s and early 1960s quickly replaced the hat.

The seemingly endless list of different hat types can be daunting, so most collectors choose to specialize in a certain style, era, or nationality of hat or at least limit their whims to either men's or women's hat styles. In men's hats, bowlers, homburgs, and tam-o'-shanters are popular American dress hat collectibles; collectors of women's hats often dote on profile hats, tricorns, or 1920s-style cloche hats.

Vintage hats can be found at estate sales, yard sales, flea markets, and thrift shops. Also, vintage clothing shows often travel to large cities across the United States in the fall and early spring and usually include many varieties of antique hats. When evaluating a potential purchase, check the hat carefully for holes, needed repairs, and authenticity. The presence of a wire frame structure and hand-sewn lining (usually of black fabric) date an authentic hat as pre- or early-1920s and, along with high-quality condition and original trimmings, will increase the hat's collectible value.

The presence of a famous milliner or couturier label such as Jay-Thorpe or Hattie Carnegie escalates a hat's value to that of a highly-prized collectible or possibly even a museum-quality item. Two labels were usually sewn into the better-quality hats—the store's label and the milliner's label. Hand-sewn rather than glued decorations will also increase a hat's value. Prices vary drastically, but a quality chapeau can rarely be found for the price of a hat from the Sears, Roebuck's 1897 catalog: fifty cents.

As you inspect a hat, you should first consider the type and condition of the material to determine whether the hat is suitable for wearing. Velvet hats outlast most other materials. To check the quality of the velvet, fold over a corner. Less of the fabric backing will show in the best velvet hats, and the velvet will have a thick pile. Softer silks wear better and last longer than stiff silks such as taffeta, which may crack with age. Felt hats and woven straw hats should be held up to the light to check for holes or slashes. Carefully turn back the brim of a straw hat; if it crackles, move on. The hat is too brittle. A straw hat with a faded color is also an indication of lost flexibility.

If you want to purchase a hat that needs minor repairs, you may be able to mend it at home with simple materials. A slash in a straw hat can be disguised by a few stitches with an ordinary needle and thread. Holes in felt hats can be patched on the inside with felt or fabric in the same color. Additional trimmings such as ribbon rosettes and lace bands can be added to help hide a patched spot in a treasured hat. Loose fabric might be repaired by resewing or by regluing with bridal glue.

For drastic reshaping or thorough cleaning, antique hats should only be entrusted to a professional hat blocker. Crumpled trimmings or a battered fabric or fur felt hat might be revived with a hand-held clothes steamer. Wool felt hats should be ironed and brushed rather than steamed in order to retain their luster and shape.

The care and storage of your vintage hats depend on the type of collection you have acquired. Some collectors never wear their hats, while others proudly display their treasured headgear atop their heads. For hat wearers, rain must be avoided. A surprise downpour can shrink felt hats, dissolve stiffening glues in fabric hats, and cause a straw hat to completely fall apart.

Many collectors prefer hatboxes for their prize hats to protect them from light, moisture, and dust. Place the hat brim-side up and stuff the box with acid-free tissue paper. Storing a hat on its brim can warp it. Hats made of silk, fur, wool, or even feathers should be accompanied in the hatbox by a moth-repellent wrapped in a clean cloth. Other collectors prefer displaying their hats on head-shaped stands in glass-fronted cabinets. Keep your hats out of direct sunlight to avoid fading. Hat hooks are generally not recommended for hat storage because they can stretch the hat.

Hat collectors regretfully acknowledge that hats no longer dominate the fashion world. A hatted head, however, always makes an exciting fashion statement; the rest of the collection is a charming addition to anyone's home decor, whether in a cabinet or resting snugly in decorative hatboxes. And who knows? Hats may be back in style tomorrow, since fashions change "at the drop of a hat."

My Mother's Lovely Face

Shirley Ruth Boyd

My mother's face is lovely,
And it will always be.
Her sun-bronzed skin is soft and smooth
And beautiful to me.

Her blue eyes, filled with love-light,
Show wisdom, faith, and mirth.
Her character of strength and love
Has guided me since birth.

Her gentleness in troubled times,
Her help in times of need.
She never said "I told you so"
Of advice I didn't heed.

She spoke with such encouragement
If I faltered on my way;

I'd go on with renewed strength,
Enlightened and so gay.

This world would be a better place
If there were more like her.
I'm sure if you could meet her once,
You'd readily concur.

Though now I journey other paths
Where fate leads me to roam,
I always feel so wonderful
Each time I go back home.

Home isn't any certain house
Or any certain place;
I know I'm home when I can see
My mother's lovely face.

26

Mother's Love

Mamie Collins Barry

From the pages of earth's annals gleam the fairest of the fair.
Flash the helmets of bold soldiers, rise the standards here and there;
Till we feel the mighty impulse of their teachings, wide and deep,
Grasping all the strength about us in their universal sweep.
How we read them, know them, love them, kiss the soft and queenly hand,
Praise the fighter, statesman, poet, and the good for which they stand!
All the forces that surround us telling what our lives shall be,
Each a partial service renders to the master unity.

But there's one whose touch is gentle, one whose power none can frame;
Poet's lore or tender fancy can but echo soft the name—
Mother's love that rocks the cradle, steers a bark on life's rough sea,
Mother's heartthrob for her offspring and her simple piety.

As the bud's exhaling fragrance hides the fullness of the flower
Till a day of revelation, with its sweet unfolding hour;
So they linger in the shadows till the time is opportune
For the priceless gems of promise to perfect their added bloom.

Mother's thoughts have permeated all the better things of earth;
To the greatest and the strongest mother's pulse has given birth.
Mother's hands have left their love prints on life's strange and tangled way;
Mother's love still guides our footsteps through the long and busy day.

NANCY SKARMEAS

MARY CASSATT
Painter

Mary Cassatt's tender and elegant paintings of mothers and their children are among the most cherished images in American art, although the artist herself was never a mother.

Consumed by her art, she faced great obstacles in her quest to become a painter. First, her family objected to her chosen profession, believing it to be unsuited for a woman; second, her native Pennsylvania offered little quality instruction; and third, once she had made it to Europe to study the best paintings and the best artists in the world, she faced doubt and condescension from her male contemporaries. "I will not admit," said the great Impressionistic painter Edgar Degas upon seeing one of Cassatt's drawings in 1874, "that a woman can draw like that." But Mary Cassatt was determined and single-minded. Through a devoted course of study and practice, she taught herself to paint and was in her own day accepted among the elite group of Impressionists that revolutionized the art world. Today, the works of Mary Cassatt hang in the world's prestigious art museums, and she is counted among the most talented of Americans ever to take up a brush.

Born in May of 1844 in Allegheny City, Pennsylvania, Mary Cassatt was seven years old when her successful father left his business to take the family on a four-year trip abroad. The Cassatts visited Paris, Heidelberg, and Darmstadt and toured the best art museums in Europe along the way. Young Mary was moved by what she saw in those museums; and upon the family's return to Pennsylvania, she announced her intention to become an artist. In 1861, she enrolled in the Pennsylvania Academy of the Fine Arts, despite the strong objections of her father. Four years later, uninspired by the instruction she was receiving at the Academy, Mary resolved to return to Europe to study independently. This intention too met with disapproval, but her mind was made up. In 1866, at the age of twenty-two, Mary sailed alone for Paris.

For the remainder of her life, Mary Cassatt was to live and paint in and around Paris, although she would make several return visits to America. She was not, however, an overnight success. Her early works were stiff and derivative; only as the years passed and her confidence grew did her unique style emerge. Mary was self-taught—she toured museums, painted in her studio, and traveled the countryside sketching. She immersed herself in the best paintings the world had to offer and devoted her time to a disciplined schedule of painting and drawing. By 1874, her work caught the eye of Degas, who, although skeptical of women's ability in general, was eventually impressed enough to invite Mary to join his group of painters, known as the Impressionists. As a member of this elite group, Mary began to build a reputation on a par with that of Degas, Camille Pissarro, Paul Gauguin, and others. In 1876, her work was exhibited in America. Mary's paintings were the first Impressionistic works to be seen on this side of the Atlantic.

It was in the 1880s that the maternal theme began to dominate in Mary's work. She had always used her family members as models. During an extended visit with her brother and his family, she found inspiration in her many nieces and nephews. Her sister, Lydia, was also a frequent model.

Mary painted the world around her—the homes she lived in, her gardens, her family members. Her paintings are beautiful and touching, and her timeless images of mother and child today remain among the most reproduced images in American art. The work of Mary Cassatt had a profound influence on her native country, even though she lived most of her productive years across the Atlantic. Her paintings were the first to expose Americans to the new style of the Impressionists, and she herself directed many prominent American collectors in their search for quality art work. One of those collectors was Louisine Havemeyer, whose extensive collection now hangs in New York's Metropolitan Museum of Art.

Mary Cassatt continued painting until the early twentieth century, when eye trouble and diabetes left her unable to work. In her thirty years of active work, she never painted a commissioned portrait and took no students; her ideas about her art were strong and personal, and she felt she could neither paint to suit the tastes of another nor impose her tastes on a developing artist. Mary Cassatt died in France in 1926. She had been gifted with a great natural talent, but like so many women of her era, she also needed an exceptional strength of character and an unwavering commitment to her work in order to succeed in a field and a world dominated by men. Her paintings are treasured for their celebration of the mother and child; her life story is a monument to strong, independent, American women.

Golden Moments

Hazel N. Scott

We walked along a well-worn trail,
   My little ones and I.
We stopped to watch a chipmunk play
   And airplanes in the sky.

We crossed a stream on mossy rocks
   To reach the other side;
For that is where the groundhog ran
   Beneath the brush to hide.

We saw the crows fly overhead
   And heard their mating call.
We gathered flowers from their bed.
   (We didn't pick them all.)

For we'd return another day
   To sit awhile and dream,
To watch the squirrels and chipmunks play
   While birds drink from the stream.

Now the sun long shadows casts;
   We must climb the hill.
Another golden moment past;
   For time will not stand still.

Readers' Reflections

Editor's Note: Readers are invited to submit unpublished, original poetry for possible publication in future issues of Ideals. Please send copies only; manuscripts will not be returned. Writers receive $10 for each published submission. Send material to Readers' Reflections, Ideals Publications Inc., P.O. Box 148000, Nashville, TN 37214-8000.

Good Night, Little One

Get into your little bed,
On your pillow lay your head,
Close your eyes and say your prayers,
Good night, little one.

Mother loves you, Daddy too,
Pretty child with eyes of blue.
Soon you'll be asleep once more,
Good night, little one.

In the morning when it's light,
And sun shines in your window bright;
You'll get up and play, but now,
Good night, little one.

Go to sleep and dream sweet dreams
Of starry nights and pale moonbeams.
Angels watch you through the night,
Good night, little one.

Sharon Patterson Stanley
Ashland, Virginia

Through a Child's Eyes

Laughter escapes
Through rosebud lips
As he stands teasingly
With hands on hips.

Sunlight sparkles
Inside bright eyes,
And love shines all around
Amid candor-filled sighs.

Little one tumbling by
Scampering busily,
Merrily spinning about
To dance staggering dizzily.

My arms outstretched
With heart opened wide
So I might see the glittering world
Through a child's eyes.

Tammy K. Mosley
Evansville, Indiana

For Sally

Hello, my darling!
My sunshine, my pride!
Come smile for your mother,
Come on, open wide!

My goodness, my gracious!
Just what can that be?
Is that one little tooth
And another I see?

Soon you'll be talking
And walking, you know!
Then reading and writing—
How fast you will grow!

Before I say "rabbit"
You'll fly from the nest.
I'll shed buckets of tears,
But it will be for the best.

But just now you're my darling!
My own little pearl!
My own little sweetheart!
My own little girl!

Larah C. Fitzwater
Tyler, Texas

Treasures

He brought me a leaf in his pudgy hand,
A gift it was plain to see;
And the joy that he gave was a gift of love,
For he is a treasure to me.

He brought me a feather, a rock, a flower,
Treasures to see and admire;
And the smile on his face as he offered them
Was everything I could desire.

He brings me more treasures each time he comes—
A worm, a seed, or a bug;
And the light in his eyes always sparkles with fun
And brings my response of a hug.

God, lead him gently and teach him well
Through treasures you guide him to see,
For the joy that he gives is a gift of love
'Cause he is a treasure to me.

Betty Ekiss
Moweaqua, Illinois

What Mothers Can Do

John C. Bonser

Mothers can do such wonderful things:
Make homes seem like castles worthy of kings,

Create an adventure by reading a book,
Smiling to show us how heaven must look.

Mothers can heal when a little heart "breaks,"
Banish "starvation" with cookies and cakes.

Mothers can judge each disputed case,
Forgiving the culprits, the docket erase.

Mothers are misers who hoard baby shoes,
Snapshots, report cards, and things others lose.

Mothers can teach in their own special school,
"Follow yellow brick roads and the wise golden rule!"

Surely mothers are angels sent here from above
To help us to soar on the wings of their love.

What Children Can Do

John C. Bonser

Children can do such incredible things:
    Multiply joys that each holiday brings,
Take us to places our memories renew
    Picnics and train rides and trips to the zoo.
Children can give us a "jelly-sweet" kiss,
    Show us a love we would otherwise miss.
Children are mirrors reflecting our youth,
    Minds filled with wonder, eyes searching for truth.
Children can bring back the dreams we once had,
    Investments in hope for tomorrows made glad.
Children can help as grandparents grow old,
    Changing their aging to pages of gold.
Naughty sometimes, yet angelic in sleep,
    Fragments of heaven ours briefly to keep.

WOMEN AIR FORCE SERVICE PILOTS. Camp Davis, North Carolina, 1943. Photograph courtesy of the National Archives.

VETERAN WOMEN READY FOR CAREERS

WASHINGTON, D.C.—Women of the armed services will face problems of career readjustment on their return to civilian life, but no one should make the mistake of considering these veterans in the "problem" category. This fundamental point was emphasized yesterday at the Conference on Postwar Career Problems of Service Women, called by Miss Margaret Hickey, President of the National Federation of Business and Professional Women's Clubs, and held at the Statler Hotel.

These women, it was pointed out, will come back into civilian life at the end of the war with broadened experience, added skills, resourcefulness, adaptability, and other qualities of character that equip them to make a continuing contribution to the nation. The problem lies in helping to direct them into fields where maximum use can be made of their ability.

RIGHT TO WORK
Public sanction of women's right to work regardless of marital status will have an important bear-

ing on the employment situation they face when they leave the service—and this concerns all women, not just women veterans, it was agreed.

Miss Hickey was unable to be present at the session, as she is remaining in San Francisco during the Security Conference. Miss Rochelle Gachet, of Alabama State College for Women, National Chairman of Education and Vocation for the B. & P.W. Federation, presided. Heads of the various women's services—Colonel Oveta Culp Hobby, director of the WAC (Women's Army Corps); Captain Dorothy C. Stratton, Director of the SPARS [S(emper) Par(atus), meaning always prepared]; Colonel Ruth Cheney Streeter, Director of the Women Marines; Commander Tova P. Wiley, Assistant Director of the WAVES (Women Accepted for Volunteer Emergency Service); Lieut. Colonel Mary G. Phillips of the Army Nurse Corps; Major Helen C. Burns, Director of Dietitians, Army Nurse Corps; and Captain Edna Lura, Assistant Director, Physical Therapy Aides—sat around the table to discuss the problems ahead.

Each of the heads of women's services answered the following four questions: What have women members of the armed forces gained in training and experience? How will that experience affect their careers? What adjustment problems are likely to arise, and what facilities will be necessary to meet them? What plans have the armed services developed to help solve the problems of readjustment?

EXPERIENCE VALUABLE
In every branch of the service, it was agreed, the women have made gains that will translate quickly into efficiency on a civilian job. The Army and Navy's responsibility for counseling ends when the veteran has her discharge papers. At the separation centers there are trained counselors who help with decisions concerning educational training or the general field of work to be taken up or resumed in civilian life. If further help is needed—and often it will be—it must be sought from civilian agencies set up for that purpose. Some concern

was expressed as to the quality of the counseling provided by these agencies. The need for well-trained and thoroughly-informed counselors on education and work was emphasized. The B. & P.W. Clubs can and will give assistance in surveying the community for job opportunities and offering counseling service also wherever possible, Miss Gachet stated. Its members are in a position to give practical help.

SPECIAL PRIVILEGES
Servicemen must report to their draft boards promptly on their return home, but a servicewoman is not obligated to do so, although this procedure is necessary if she desires to return to her former job. This is one of her privileges under the G. I. Bill of Rights, as are maintenance of her seniority and insurance benefits. Major Marian C. Lichty of the Veterans Personnel Division, Selective Service, pointed out the importance of a woman veteran taking advantage of these rights. "The veteran should be looked upon as an asset to the community—returning with something to give," Major Lichty added.

The SPARS have twelve discharge centers where both men and women are demobilized and given counseling aid. If the Women Marines are looking for new jobs and do not find them, they may apply for further assistance to their branch of the service even after their discharge.

Miss Frances Maule, editor of the B. & P.W. magazine *Independent Woman* gave the summary of the morning discussion. Miss Gachet, closing the afternoon session, defined the purpose of the B. & P.W. Federation to help develop public opinion that would encourage women veterans to inform themselves about opportunities open to them, to see that services for giving such information function adequately, and to keep informed on the programs for the retraining and readjustment of both men and women veterans.

Originally printed in The Christian Science Monitor, *May 17, 1945.*

In Mother's Heart

Mamie Ozburn Odum

When I was but a little child,
I heard my mother's name.
Then I heard them speak of God
And thought they were the same.

They said that God was very good
And loved all children truly;
My mother loved me day and night
And counseled when unruly.

They promised God would care for me;
He did, but she did too.
I took my childish wants to her;
My joys and hurts she knew.

Then on I grew to womanhood
And found the two apart
But feel I was not very wrong —
God dwelled in Mother's heart.

40

A SLICE OF LIFE

— Edgar A. Guest —

MOTHER'S JOB

I'm just the man to make things right,
To mend a sleigh or make a kite,
Or wrestle on the floor and play
Those rough and tumble games, but say!
Just let him get an ache or pain
And start to whimper and complain,
And from my side he'll quickly flee
To clamber on his mother's knee.

I'm good enough to be his horse
And race with him along the course.
I'm just the friend he wants each time
There is a tree he'd like to climb,
And I'm the pal he's eager for

When we approach the candy store;
But for his mother straight he makes
Whene'er his little stomach aches.

He likes, when he is feeling well,
The kind of stories that I tell;
And I'm his comrade and his chum,
And I must march behind his drum.
To me through thick and thin he'll stick,
Unless he happens to be sick.
In which event, with me he's through—
Only his mother then will do.

Edgar A. Guest began his illustrious career in 1895 at the age of fourteen when his work first appeared in the Detroit Free Press. *His column was syndicated in over 300 newspapers, and he became known as "The Poet of the People."*

Little Bo Peep and Angel Rides

Micki Warner

In the eighth grade play, I got a starring role. It wasn't the lead, because the lead was Humpty Dumpty, and that role went to an eighth grade boy, a large one. I was Little Bo Peep and the most envied second grader in the Saint Boniface school. Magnificent acting talents did not land me this treasured role. I got the part because I had the longest, blondest hair of any kid in Saint Boniface. Plays also require costumes, and my mother could sew like a bandit. Nuns are smart.

For two months of dress rehearsals, I danced and smiled my head off. My mother created elaborate and beautiful costumes under the direction of Sisters Marie and Bernadette. Mine was a perfect period piece complete with a pinafore, pantaloons, and a perky bonnet that framed my long blond curls. A wonderful herding crook adorned with ribbons and flowers completed my Bo Peep ensemble.

The night of the play, my mother frantically put the finishing touches on all of the costumes. My anxiety was intense—becoming a star was strenuous and exhausting. My older brother, also an "entertainer," offered me his famous "angel ride" for stress reduction. Our angel rides worked as follows: my brother lay on his back with his knees drawn to his chest. I carefully balanced myself on his feet. As he cried "take off!" my brother flung his legs straight up into the air, which sent me flying across the room. Usually I landed on the couch, but this particular night my landing gear failed. I hit a chair, face first, and blood went everywhere. My cowardly brother bolted from the room to leave my horrified mother with the gruesome task of face repair.

The cut over my eye wasn't bad. It could be hidden by the perky bonnet and masses of blond hair. The fat lip was another matter. After my mother applied some ice, I stopped bleeding and bawling and managed to wash my face. With fresh makeup (extra on the lip), we left for the play. The nuns were horrified, but they still let me go on. The play was a success. I was a star, and no one commented on the fat lip of Bo Peep.

Days later, I heard my mother talking to one of her friends on the telephone. I heard her say, "Thank God she didn't have a speaking part." I was stunned. It never occurred to me that a "speaking part" was something important for a beautiful, blond-haired actress like me. That was the first of many lessons I learned from my mother.

THROUGH MY WINDOW

Pamela Kennedy

Art by Russ Flint

FIELD TRIP FOLLIES

It's that time of year again when every mother receives tender notes of love and appreciation, bouquets of fragrant spring blossoms, and a plea to help chaperone the class field trip. When the weather begins to warm, teachers eagerly plan excursions for their charges to "broaden their horizons" and give them "hands on" experiences in the museums and marshes of America.

Of course no teacher in her right mind

would venture forth by herself with a few dozen children, so the draft notices come home to mothers everywhere. My first two offsprings were boys, and they begged me not to answer the field trip call. In fact, my oldest son once refused to attend his own class field trip when he found I was planning to go. I declined and left him to some other intrepid chaperone. But when my daughter entered school, it was her desire that I attend every event the teacher planned. I tried to be selective but have been to more class field trips than I care to recall.

I am a person who likes to know what is going to happen. I like to have a plan and to have the plan followed. Field trips, however, defy the best laid plans. No matter how detailed your instructions, how orderly your preparation, how clear your directions, something always goes wrong. Often it involves the bus. The day of the field trip, the bus usually arrives late. If it is on time, the driver isn't sure of the directions to the field trip site or makes a few wrong turns, so you inevitably arrive at your destination tardy and apologetic. This causes the tour guide to openly glance at her watch and frown at the chaperones, as if they had somehow plotted to be late and ruin her schedule. A cranky field trip guide is not a good beginning to a fun day.

People who lead field trips through museums and historical sites rarely seem to understand that lots of historical background just doesn't interest most elementary school children. Guides who dress in period costumes invariably are asked whether or not they are wearing old-fashioned underwear too and if their hair is real or fake. The group I accompanied to George Washington's home in Mount Vernon, Virginia, was much more interested in George and Martha's lack of plumbing facilities than where they entertained General Lafayette! In addition, the children were enchanted with a demonstration of how the field hands had to squash tobacco worms with their bare hands, but the kids couldn't have cared less about the Constitutional Convention! It is difficult, as a mother, to maintain a sense of decorum when the children, recognized as "yours" by the docent, make inappropriate remarks about the father of our country!

If you accompany children to any type of outdoor excursion, plan to get wet. Most children seem drawn to water like moths to a flame. I'm not sure why, but rarely do teachers instruct children to bring extra clothes. This means that after Rebecca falls into the fountain, she must depend upon the generosity and creativity of her mother-chaperone for dry clothes. I'm still missing a sweatshirt worn as a dress by a drenched first grader.

A truly organized teacher hands out assignments on the way to the field trip so that her students will spend their field trip time wisely and read all the information posted by each exhibit. That's what is supposed to happen. What really happens is this: the class "star" zooms through the assignment and fills in all of the blanks correctly while his or her classmates dash around like gerbils in a maze. On the way home, the panicked "gerbils" call out the questions to one another on the bus, corporately filling the blanks with the majority opinion. Some of the field trip chaperone mothers feel it is their duty to see that their group comes back to school with neat papers, correctly filled in. I am of the opinion that if I get back on the bus with the same number of kids I started with, the trip was a smashing success.

Perhaps this is why the children in the other mothers' groups were busy writing reports on the history of pre-Columbian art while my group was just finishing up their "sorry" letters to the docent at the Smithsonian. Although we had a very enlightening time, the teacher tactfully suggested that I might like to help out at sports day next year and give another mother the opportunity to go on a field trip. I tried to sound reluctant as I agreed. "Yes," I said with a sigh, "I can see where we really ought to share the wealth."

Pamela Kennedy is a freelance writer of short stories, articles, essays, and children's books. Wife of a naval officer and mother of three children, she has made her home on both U.S. coasts and currently resides in Honolulu, Hawaii. She draws her material from her own experiences and memories, adding highlights from her imagination to enhance the story.

My Garden

Mary Ramthun Young

Once it was but barren land,
Just a bit of clay and sand.
So with spade I planted trees,
Flowering shrubs for birds and bees,
Planted grass and bulbs and seeds,
Spaded, hoed, and pulled out weeds.
Where it once was brown and bare,
I now have a garden there.

Larkspur, blue beside the wall,
Hollyhocks so straight and tall,
Columbine and poppies bright
Glow beside the daisies white.
Here and there the bluebells nod
And above, the goldenrod.
All my garden blooms so fair
Where 'twas once so brown and bare.

O'er a trellis hangs a vine;
From a pool the lilies shine.
In the trees the robins sing
Songs and melodies of spring;
Everywhere is music gay,
Chasing every cloud away.
Blue and clear the sky above,
All my garden whispers love.

WISHING

William Allingham

Ring-ting! I wish I were a primrose,
A bright yellow primrose blowing in the spring!
    The stooping bough above me,
    The wandering bee to love me,
The fern and moss to creep across,
    And the elm tree for our king!

Nay-stay! I wish I were an elm tree,
A great, lofty elm tree with green leaves gay!
    The winds would set them dancing;
    The sun and moonshine glance in;
And the birds would house among the boughs
    And sweetly sing.

Oh, no! I wish I were a robin—
A robin or a little wren, everywhere to go,
    Through forest, field, or garden
    And ask no leave or pardon
Till winter comes with icy thumbs
    To ruffle up our wings!

Well, tell! Where should I fly to?
Where go sleep in the dark wood or dell?
    Before the day was over,
    Home must come the rover
For Mother's kiss—sweeter this
    Than any other thing.

The unique perspective of Russ Flint's artistic style has made him a favorite of Ideals *readers for many years. A resident of California and father of four, Russ Flint has illustrated a children's Bible and many other books.*

My Mother's Quilt

Margaret Rushmer

My mother cut the pieces
And sewed them one by one
Into a lovely pattern
Until the quilt was done.

With pieces bright and glowing
And some a duller shade,
The quilt brought out the colors
Of flowers in our glade.

I see her face before me,
With eyes and cheeks aglow.
The needle swiftly threaded,
She made the quilt soon grow.

She pieced the top together,
Then placed it on the white;
And 'neath her nimble fingers,
The blocks were done by night.

At last the quilt was finished,
A gift of stitches fine;
And breathlessly we looked on
Her quilt sewn in love-time.

Opposite Page
QUILT WITH ANTIQUE SIDEBOARD
Jessie Walker Associates

Handmade Heirloom

Mary Skarmeas

LINENS EMBELLISHED WITH CROCHETED EDGING. Jerry Koser Photography.

CROCHETED EDGING

The craft of crochet has a long and uncertain history. Although remnants of crude, ancient forms of crochet have been unearthed in the Middle East, China, and the American Southwest, the first significant information about crocheting comes from middle Europe. During the Renaissance, the art of making lace from fine thread worked with tiny, hooked needles enjoyed a short period of popularity in Belgium, France, England, and Italy. During this time the name "crochet" first appeared, derived from the French word *croc*, meaning hook, which referred to the small, hooked needle that is the tool of all crocheting.

Interest in crocheting waned, however, until the mid-nineteenth century, when upper-class English women rediscovered the craft. These women developed endless variations on the basic technique of crocheted lace-making and with practice, imagination, and endless hours of leisure found the possible stitch combinations and patterns unlimited.

About the same time as the women of England were rediscovering the art of crochet, the devastation of the potato famine was spreading across the countryside of Ireland. The farm families of Ireland, deprived of their main source of livelihood, fell into extreme poverty. As a gesture of charity, a group of English women made efforts to introduce crochet to the women of Ireland, hoping to give birth to a cottage industry that might provide some new source of income. Obviously, crocheted lace was not the answer to the problems of the Irish people, but the craft took hold, and Irish women began to develop their own unique, delicate, lace patterns. Crafted out of fine linen thread with the slimmest of needles, "Irish crochet," or "Irish lace," became known throughout Europe and is still produced in many Irish villages today.

This type of crochet work was perfect for edging household linens such as napkins, tablecloths, guest towels, sheets, and pillowcases. Today, a delicate lace edge, carefully hand crocheted using the stitches and patterns developed by the women of Ireland, recalls a time gone by and adds a touch of grace and elegance to our homes; handmade edging turns a common household item into an heirloom craft.

Patterns for all types of crochet are as near as your local library or bookstore, and instructions with detailed illustrations are easy to follow. From the very simplest edging to the most intricate designs, there is something for every taste and every level of ability. A ball of thread or yarn, a crochet hook, a basic, interlocking stitch, and your own time, patience, and imagination can create beautiful items for your home—gifts or one-of-a-kind treasures to pass on to future generations.

My own experience with crochet is limited, but I do remember my first lesson, given by one of my older sisters many years ago. She taught me the basic stitches and then gave me a ball of fine pastel crochet thread, a slim hooked needle, and a dainty linen handkerchief prepunched with tiny holes around the edges. With patience and care she helped me turn a plain white handkerchief into something unique and beautiful. This simple but satisfying success instilled in me a love of all needlework that has, throughout my life, provided many hours of relaxation and satisfaction.

My interests today run more to knitting and sewing, but all needleworkers can take inspiration from the crocheted lace edgings perfected by the women of nineteenth-century Ireland. We all have baskets, boxes, or trunks filled with an accumulation of odds and ends—fabric pieces, ribbon, lace, and more—that are too good to throw away. My mother had a scarred and battered old steamer trunk that crossed the ocean with some anxious, excited relative on his or her way to the New World and a new life. This wonderful treasure chest held strips of wool cut from old coats, waiting to be braided; scraps of calico and other cotton fabric that would one day be quilts; mason jars filled with old buttons; and boxes of ribbon, lace, and rickrack that would some day add a finishing touch to a handmade garment.

I too have a basket full of remnants waiting for that "special project." In light of what I have learned about crocheted edgings, my basket now seems full of potential. Edging, after all, can be made of almost anything. Strips of fine lace, alternated with narrow satin ribbon, can be sewn on top of a pillowcase border. Gathered crochet borders on guest towels might create a romantic effect. Wide scalloped lace will look lovely on the edge of a sheet. An elegant look might be achieved by inserting a wide flat strip of sheer lace between the border and main section of a dresser scarf, letting the rich color of the wood show through. A fertile imagination, a store of scraps, and the inspiration of crocheted edging give way to endless possibilities.

The art of crocheted edging is timeless, delicate, and unique. Its basic premise may be applied to any craft materials or methods: to take something ordinary and, by your creative efforts, make it more beautiful. By adding crocheted edging to an ordinary household linen, you can create something worth holding on to through the years.

Mary Skarmeas lives in Danvers, Massachusetts, and is studying for her bachelor's degree in English at Suffolk University. Mother of four and grandmother of one, Mary loves all crafts, especially knitting.

Embroideries

Kari Sharp Hill

In the linen closet, next to the cheerful prints and modern geometrics, lie a pair of hand-embroidered pillowcases. My mother stitched this particular pair when I was nine years old. Her skilled hands fed the needle through the stiff new fabric as she created a border of bluebirds who were deftly using their gentle beaks to twist yellow ribbons into plump bows.

Often I begged her to let me try. She would smile and pull my eternal dresser scarf from her basket. With uncooperative fingers, I struggled. The thread would tangle, and gaping holes would stare up at me from all of the places where french knots should have rested. I fussed until my project was returned, unfinished, to the protection of Mother's sewing basket.

"That's enough for now," she would say. "Go enjoy the fresh air; it may rain tomorrow." I'd run outside, graciously released from my defeat.

I was fifteen the first time a boy broke my heart. I came home, dropped my coat on the sofa, and ran into my room. I crossed his name out in my diary with a black magic marker. After I cried for awhile, I decided to dedicate myself to becoming a famous writer. Through my novels, I'd make that boy pay many times over the price of being a villain.

When I came out of my room, red-eyed and resolved, I found my mother on her favorite end of the sofa stitching. A tray next to her held two glasses of ice and a rare bottle of Coca-Cola. We shared the treat while Mom worked on another pair of pillowcases.

"Mom, I'm going to be a writer," I announced.

"A writer." She tried it out on her tongue the way girls try out their boyfriends' last names attached to their own first names. "A writer needs a good hat," she said with a grin.

"What kind of hat?" I asked.

She started stitching again. "A big hat with lots of fruit or flowers on it," she said, "something you'd never wear in public, a hat to wear when you're thinking up stories in your room." She glanced up from her work and punctuated the air with her needle. "My aunt Sally had a hat like that. She wrote novels."

MARBLE BARS

In a medium mixing bowl, cream 1 cup butter or margarine and 2 cups firmly-packed brown sugar. Add 2 eggs and 2 teaspoons vanilla; mix well. In a separate mixing bowl, sift together 2½ cups flour, 1 teaspoon baking soda, and 1 teaspoon salt. Add dry ingredients to butter mixture; mix well. Stir in 3 cups quick-cooking rolled oats (uncooked). Set aside.

In a small saucepan, combine one 12-ounce package of semisweet chocolate chips, one 14-ounce can of sweetened condensed milk, 2 tablespoons butter or margarine, and ½ teaspoon salt. Melt over low heat, stirring occasionally. Remove from heat; stir in 1 cup chopped nuts and 2 teaspoons vanilla.

Spread ⅔ batter in a greased jelly-roll pan. Cover with chocolate mixture. Dot with remaining batter and use a wooden spoon to swirl topping and create marbleized effect. Bake in a preheated 350° F oven for 25 to 30 minutes.

Margaret Helen Wallace
Winnebago, Minnesota

CHOCOLATE PEANUT BUDDY BARS

In a large mixing bowl, combine 1 cup creamy peanut butter and 6 tablespoons softened butter or margarine; cream until fluffy. Add 1¼ cups granulated sugar, 3 eggs, and 1 teaspoon vanilla; beat well. Stir in 1 cup flour and ¼ teaspoon salt. Add 1 cup milk chocolate morsels; mix well.

Spread the batter into an ungreased 9- x 13- x 2-inch pan. Bake in a preheated 350° F oven for 25 to 30 minutes or until edges begin to brown.

In a small saucepan, melt an additional 1 cup milk chocolate morsels with an additional ½ cup creamy peanut butter. Spread topping evenly over the bars. Cool completely. Makes 48 bars.

Christine A. Koskey
Wausau, Wisconsin

BROWN SUGAR BARS

In a mixing bowl, sift together ⅔ cup flour, 1 teaspoon baking powder, and ¼ teaspoon salt. Set aside.

In a large saucepan, melt ¼ cup margarine. Remove from heat, and stir in 1 cup firmly-packed brown sugar. Add 1 egg and 1 teaspoon vanilla; beat well. Add ½ cup chopped nuts. Stir in dry ingredients. Spread the batter in a greased 8-inch square baking pan. Bake in a preheated 350° F oven for 20 to 25 minutes. Cut into bars immediately and cool. Makes 16 bars.

Olive Wetherington
Lake City, Florida

GRANDMOTHER

Jane Smallwood

About Grandmother
I could write a book
but will just look
at one memory.

It was how she could bake
a blackberry jam cake.
We could hardly wait
for the slicing
through the
luscious caramel icing.

And the blackberry jam
was finger-licking
as we recalled the fun
of berry picking.

FOOD FOR THOUGHT

June Masters Bacher

I'm a mixture of cook and teacher.
"But which do you teach?" ask they.
"I teach small children," I tell them,
"To measure their work and their play."
"Will you share the recipe with us?"
"I'm no formula person," I say.
"Each takes a special blending,
And ingredients change some each day:
One child needs sorting and sifting;
Another a gentle pat;
But all need a dash of affection.
They simply won't rise without that!"
So with courage and sometimes misgiving,
I roll up my sleeves and begin
That special gourmet assignment
Of molding gingerbread boys into men.

Simple Things

Marcia Krugh Leaser

It never took important things
    To make my mother glad.
She always seemed so satisfied
    With the "simple things" she had.

It mattered not the vase was cracked
    Or the picture had a flaw.
She proudly sat it on the table
    Or displayed it on the wall.

She was the same with people too,
    Accepting all for who they were,
Allowing them to be themselves
    When visiting with her.

Her friends were always many,
    Be they rich or be they poor,
Knowing that a friendly welcome
    Would be waiting at her door.

I always envied Mother
    For her eyes that did not see
The many flaws in "simple things"
    That were so plain to me.

I only pray with age that I
    Will learn to be as she
Because I know a blessing lies
    In her philosophy.

BITS & PIECES

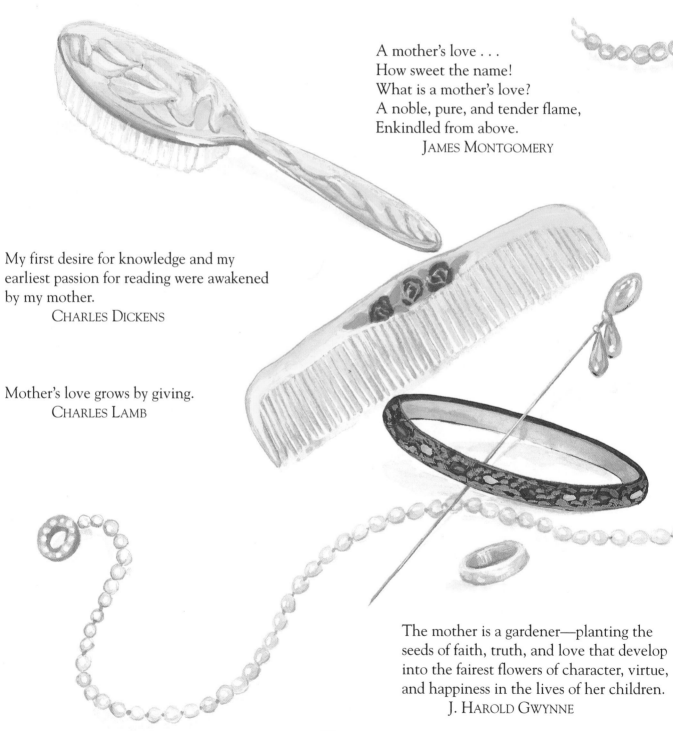

A mother's love . . .
How sweet the name!
What is a mother's love?
A noble, pure, and tender flame,
Enkindled from above.
JAMES MONTGOMERY

My first desire for knowledge and my
earliest passion for reading were awakened
by my mother.
CHARLES DICKENS

Mother's love grows by giving.
CHARLES LAMB

The mother is a gardener—planting the
seeds of faith, truth, and love that develop
into the fairest flowers of character, virtue,
and happiness in the lives of her children.
J. HAROLD GWYNNE

A mother is a mother still,
the holiest thing alive.
SAMUEL TAYLOR COLERIDGE

There is no velvet as soft as Mother's lap,
no rose as lovely as her smile, no path as
flowery as that imprinted with her footsteps.
ARCHBISHOP THOMSON

When a child was asked
 "Where is your home?" she replied,
"Wherever my mother is, is my home."
AUTHOR UNKNOWN

Love droops; youth fades;
The leaves of friendship fall;
A mother's love outlives them all.
OLIVER WENDELL HOLMES

Never comes mortal utterance so near
to eternity as when a child utters words
of loving praise to a mother. Every syllable
drops into the jewel box of her memory,
to be treasured forever.
LYON

May Is a Song

Loise Pinkerton Fritz

May is a song, is a song, is a song
With lyrics of jubilant spring:
The dawning of warmth, the budding of flowers,
The north-coming birds on the wing.

The peepers a-peeping a chorus of cheer,
The brooklets devoid of all ice,
The grasses a-dressing in green finery;
May is a song of delight.

May is a song, is a song, is a song,
The sweetest of all roundelays;
A chorus of fond repetition,
Resounding forth day after day.

A tune that is old, yet as new as each spring,
A strain that is welcome each year.
May is a song, is a song, is a song,
Sweet music to each listening ear.

Overnight Magic

Carice Williams

I thought for sure that Spring would not
Come back to us this year,
For nowhere could I find the signs
That she would soon appear.

Yet overnight the magic came,
And like a happy dream
Spring waved her wand and brought to life
Each valley, field, and stream.

The lilac and the hawthorn hedge
Today burst forth in bloom,
And pale primroses by the gate
Soon chase out winter's gloom.

All nature comes to life once more
When gardeners work the sod.
We credit Springtime for the change
When actually it's God.

AZALEAS AT CALLAWAY GARDENS. Pine Mountain, Georgia. Dick Dietrich Photography.

CALLAWAY GARDENS
Pine Mountain, Georgia

Secluded in the pine forests of south-west Georgia, Callaway Gardens is a nature lover's paradise. The mission statement of Callaway Gardens is to "provide a wholesome family environment where all may find beauty, relaxation, inspiration, and a better understanding of the living world." Callaway Gardens is the result of one man's vision to spread the love of nature to all people. Through the efforts of Cason J. Callaway and his wife, Virginia, Callaway Gardens has become a family resort geared toward education, meditation, and just plain old fun!

Today the resort encompasses more than 14,000 acres in the area surrounding Pine Mountain, Georgia. Attractions include the Cecil B. Day Butterfly Center, the John A. Sibley Horticultural Center, Mr. Cason's Vegetable Garden, the Discovery Bicycle Trail, the Ida Cason Memorial Chapel, the Pioneer Log Cabin, and seemingly endless miles of winding trails through the expansive, wooded gardens. All of the many components within Callaway are managed under the guidance of the Ida B. Callaway Foundation, which is dedicated, like the chapel, to

Cason's mother whom he felt sparked his love of nature.

Callaway Gardens offers a variety of accommodations that cater to the many needs of its guests. Visitors can rent country cottages, enjoy luxurious Mountain Creek Villas, or rest comfortably in the Callaway Gardens Inn. Once settled, it will be difficult to decide which activity to do first! Mountain Creek Lake offers 175 acres for bass, bream, and other recreational fishing. Paddle boats, sailboats, and canoes are available for rent, and other diversions include championship golf courses such as the Mountain View course, which serves as the site for the Professional Golf Association's Buick Southern Open. Callaway Gardens also offers a five-star tennis center, racquetball courts, a lake-side jogging trail, and 1,000 acres of hunting reserve.

Perhaps the most fascinating attraction in the Gardens is the Cecil B. Day Butterfly Center. Opened in 1988 as the largest glass-enclosed butterfly conservatory in North America, it has earned worldwide recognition. This amazing center is home to more than 1,000 butterflies as well as dozens of birds. Within the glass-paneled octagon, a waterfall cascades into a pool surrounded by tropical foliage. Since education was a prime concern of Cason Callaway, the center continues his aims today; visitors are encouraged to view an introductory video on butterflies before entering the conservatory. Afterward guests may stroll through the one-and-a-half acres of gardens specially designed to attract butterflies, and workshops are available for those visitors interested in starting their own butterfly gardens.

In a continuing effort to study the natural environment, the John A. Sibley Horticultural Center is a main attraction at Callaway Gardens. The center consists of five acres of carefully designed plantings that integrate the indoor and outdoor environments. Created ten years ago, it challenges the concept of the "traditional" conservatory and houses unique floral displays, greenhouses, and a twenty-two-foot waterfall and pool.

For those interested in the "fruit of the earth," Mr. Cason's Vegetable Garden offers a glimpse at new techniques and helpful hints in home gardening. Visitors may take their time strolling through the numerous plots geared toward specific cultivation including the herb garden, middle and upper terrace vegetable gardens, and the home demonstration garden where the weekly Public Broadcasting Service television show "The Victory Garden" is filmed.

For a more aerobic view of Callaway Gardens, visitors may choose to rent bicycles and cruise the Discovery Trail. More than seven miles of paths provide guests access to some of the most breathtaking scenery at Callaway. While never too far from the other attractions, the trails run next to mountain streams and amid wildlife areas to create the illusion of being miles away. At the end of the trail, guests are invited to climb aboard the ferry for a relaxing ride across Mountain Creek Lake to their starting point.

Sound tiring? Don't worry. One of the most popular activities at Callaway Gardens is just relaxing on the deck of your cottage while listening to the wind rustle the needles far above in the Georgia pines. Meditative peace can also be found in the Ida Cason Memorial Chapel on the banks of Fall Creek Lake. It is here that the vision of the Callaway family lives on. The chapel was dedicated by Dr. Norman Vincent Peale in 1962. Its stained glass windows, which represent the four seasons in the Gardens, reflect God in nature. The Moller pipe organ can be heard outside as well as inside during the many organ concerts held throughout the year.

Touched by Cason Callaway's vision of natural beauty, visitors to Callaway Gardens take with them an improved understanding and appreciation of our natural world.

*"The trees,
like the longings
of the earth,
stand atiptoe
to peep at heaven."*

—Rabindranath Tagore

BRIGHT ORCHARD BOUNTY

Elisabeth Weaver Winstead

It's an apple-blossom morning;
Pink-tipped petals dance and swing.
The dappled sun goes singing by
To light the mist-blue bowl of sky.

The fresh, sweet scent of orchard trees
Invites the hum of golden bees.
Flocks of robins swing and swoop,
As graceful as a ballet troupe.

Tall trees of apples on the hill
Shine in beauty, etched and still.
As blossomed buds on trees unfold,
They gleam in rays of purest gold.

72

HOLLYHOCK
Alcea Rosea
R. Todd Davis Photography

Hollyhock Time

Mrs. Oliver J. Saltsgiver

The bees are droning all the day;
The birds are singing loud and gay,
" 'Tis hollyhock time in Iowa."
Beside each walk and garden wall,
They stand like sentinels straight and tall;
In each nook, by the winding road,
They bend in beauty beneath their load.
And as we pass they nod and say,
"Have faith in God; be kind today;
'Tis hollyhock time in Iowa."

One with Thee

Effie Truex Cook

I could not be
A thing apart—
Aloof from You,
From skies of blue,
From flow'rs so sweet,
From every leaf
And twig and tree.

I could not be
A thing apart.
So help me be
As one with Thee
And every leaf
And twig and tree.
My thanks to Thee.

Spring in the Woods

Nina Gail Stong

Away to the woods where the shadows lie deep;
The flowers have wakened from winter's long sleep.
The air's richly laden with perfume so sweet;
A violet carpet is laid for our feet.
A green leafy arbor o'erhead stretches high;
Hear the song of the birds! See the blue of the sky!

Here's jack-in-the-pulpit with gay coat of green;
Here's a buttercup maiden, the fairest I've seen;
Here white and pure lilies and adder tongues gold;
What wonderful treasures a spring day can hold.
Here fine green umbrellas await shower fall;
Here's a toadstool to rest on, and here's a puffball.

So we wander and gather the flowers at will;
The springtime is ours, and our hearts with joy thrill.
We gather in handfuls, how eager the quest;
Flowers seen in the distance seem brightest and best.
Onward and onward to a yet fairer land,
Those picked first are withered by the warmth of the hand.

So in life's driving search for the pleasures so sweet,
In our mad rush to pluck, we miss those at our feet.

AZALEAS AT LANTERN COURT
The Holden Arboretum
Lake County, Ohio
Ian Adams Photography

Readers' Forum

Meet Our Ideals *Readers and Their Families*

ATTENTION *IDEALS* READERS: The *Ideals* editors are looking for "favorite memories" for the magazine. Please send a typed description of your favorite holiday memory or tradition to: Favorite Memories, c/o Editorial Department, Ideals Publications Inc., P.O. Box 148000, Nashville, TN 37214-8000.

CAROLYN KINNEY of Fort Walton Beach, Florida, dotes on granddaughter Casi Kinney, age three (pictured above left). Casi lives with her mother and father in Maryland, but she spent seven months with her grandmother while father Greg Kinney was being transferred from a United States Air Force base in England to the United States.

Casi loves helping her Grandmother cook and garden. Carolyn travels North to see Casi and her parents as often as possible.

Grandmother ANNA RAY of West Jefferson, North Carolina, sent us this photograph of her four-year-old grandchild Hava Brianne Romans (pictured above right), who is all dressed up for a special tea party with her grandmother and her dolls.

Anna wrote that Hava loves to dress up in grown-up clothes and even try her hand at make-up (just for fun). Hava also loves leafing through the pages of Grandmother's *Ideals!*

Breathtaking Art
Todd Palmer

When TODD PALMER of Port Orange, Florida, saw Mary Cassatt's painting *The Boating Party*, he was struck by its resemblance to the above photograph of his wife Jackie and their sleeping baby daughter, Bailey. Although Bailey and her twin sister Ragan are constant sources of inspiration, the proud father was so inspired by the photograph that he penned the following poem. Thank you, Todd, for sharing this special moment of motherhood (and fatherhood) with us.

I look at Cassatt's *Boating Party*,
And there we sit in the dining room:
At the head of the table
That's me in black
Braced for leverage,
Head cocked with intent,
Oars locked in for the long row.

As if she knows how to relax,
The child reclines,
Embraced by the wife,
Whose eyes reflect
Your secure sense of motherly content,

Though she wishes he would
Stop the headstrong push.
Why not drop the oars
Since the wind has filled
The sail with strength
Enough to keep their course?
His back is turned
To what lies ahead,
But he seems to see the future
In his daughter's carefree stare

Just as I saw it in you
Sitting there at dinner,
Cradling our sleeping daughter,
That secure sense of motherly content
Reflected in your drowsy eyes.

I had to stop eating
And savor the scene:
Our own boating party in the dining room
Where we sailed for an instant
While I paused to catch my breath.

THANK YOU Carolyn Kinney, Anna Ray, and Todd Palmer for sharing with *Ideals*. We hope to hear from other readers who would like to share photos and stories with the *Ideals* family. Please include a self-addressed, stamped envelope if you would like the photos returned. Keep your original photographs for safe-keeping and send duplicate photos along with your name, address, and telephone number to:

READERS' FORUM
IDEALS PUBLICATIONS INC.
P.O. BOX 148000
NASHVILLE, TN 37214-8000

ideals

Publisher, Patricia A. Pingry
Editor, Lisa C. Thompson
Art Director, Patrick McRae
Copy Editor, Michelle Prater Burke
Electronic Prepress Manager,
    Amilyn K. Lanning
Editorial Intern, Heather R. McArthur
Contributing Editors, Lansing Christman, Deana Deck, Russ Flint, Pamela Kennedy, Mary Skarmeas, Nancy Skarmeas

ACKNOWLEDGMENTS

FOOD FOR THOUGHT from THE GRANDMOTHER BOOK by June Masters Bacher, copyright © 1982 by June Masters Bacher. Reprinted by permission of the author. MOTHER'S JOB from THE PATH TO HOME by Edgar A. Guest, copyright © 1919 by The Reilly & Lee Co. Reprinted by permission of the author's estate. DEW from ROSES FOR REMEMBRANCE by Patience Strong, copyright © 1960 by Patience Strong, published by Frederick Muller Ltd. Reprinted by permission of Rupert Crew Limited. Our sincere thanks to the following authors selected from HOMESPUN, copyright © 1936 by American Book Company, whom we were unable to contact: Mamie Collins Barry for MOTHER'S LOVE; Effie Truex Cook for ONE WITH THEE; Caroline Darr Fitzsimmons for MEMORIES OF FIRST SPRING BLOSSOMS; Margaret Rushmer for MY MOTHER'S QUILT; Mrs. Oliver J. Saltsgiver for HOLLYHOCK TIME; Nina Gail Stong for SPRING IN THE WOODS, and Mary Ramthun Young for MY GARDEN.

★ ★ ★ VICTORY ★ ★ ★

HONORING THE 50TH ANNIVERSARY OF THE ALLIED TRIUMPH IN WORLD WAR II

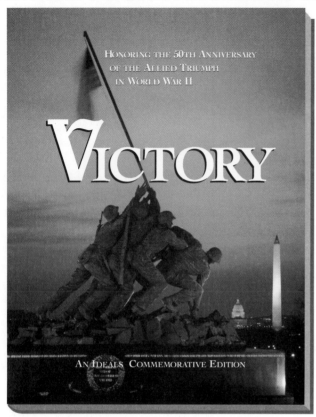

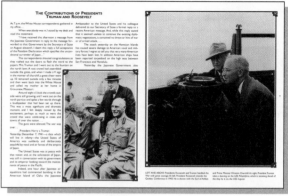

Pres. Roosevelt, left, attends the Quebec Conference of 1943; Pres. Truman, right, inspects the instruments aboard the USS Augusta.

I n this year, the fiftieth anniversary of World War II, Ideals is honored to publish a salute to the men and women who left their homes to fight and die for freedom and to those who remained behind to shoulder the load of wartime production.

OFFICIAL PHOTOGRAPHS OF THE ERA

Our editors have culled photos from the National Archives and other sources to locate moments frozen in time, some well-known and remembered, others never before published. Hum along with the tunes of Glenn Miller; stand beside the women who built the Liberty ships and bombers; and peek from the shadows as the final documents are signed that ended the long nightmare of war.

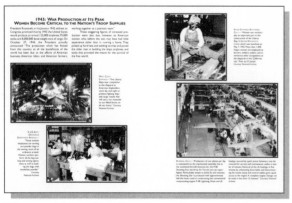

Wartime production brought mothers and wives out of the homes and into factories to build planes and ships.

REMEMBRANCES BY ORDINARY FOLKS

We've also collected some heartwarming stories from ordinary folks living in extraordinary times, such as a doctor who ministered to the sick in a Mississippi POW camp, a young Frenchwoman who spoke no English but arrived in Boston to live with her new in-laws who spoke no French, and the countless stories of rationing, bond rallies, USO dances, Red Cross volunteers, and scrap drives.

WORDS OF THE WORLD'S LEADERS

From the words of President Roosevelt on that "date which will live in infamy" to Churchill's speeches to the House of Commons to General Eisenhower's message to the troops on the eve of D-Day—these are the words and phrases that made up a lifetime.

A BOOK FOR THE WHOLE FAMILY

Young and old alike will thrill to the story of this history-making era; as older folks reminisce through the photographs of events, youngsters will learn about the heritage of their country and about a time when bravery was commonplace.

STURDY COVER AND HIGH-QUALITY PAPER

This book is of the highest production quality available, from the sturdy hardbound cover to the high quality coated stock inside; this is a collector's item to cherish for years to come.